How To Draw
Dinosaurs

How To Draw
Dinosaurs

Author
Susie Hodge

Artist
Steve Roberts

BARDFIELD
PRESS

contents

Materials ——————— 6

Shading ——————— 8

Texture ——————— 10

Perspective ——————— 12

Action ——————— 13

Brachiosaurus ——————— 14

Allosaurus ——————— 16

Herrerasaurus ——— 18

Ornithomimus ——— 20

Dilophosaurus ——— 22

Deinonychus —— 24

Polacanthus —— 26

Triceratops —— 28

Ankylosaurus —— 30

Velociraptor —— 32

Spinosaurus —— 34

Parasaurolophus — 36

Compsognathus — 38

Stegosaurus —— 40

Tyrannosaurus — 42

Gallery —— 44

materials

ALL YOU NEED TO START DRAWING IS A PENCIL AND SOME PAPER, BUT IF YOU COLLECT SOME OTHER MATERIALS AS WELL, YOU WILL BE ABLE TO CREATE EVEN MORE EXCITING EFFECTS IN YOUR DRAWINGS.

Crayons
Wax crayons can be used on their own or with other materials to produce lots of interesting results.

Coloured pencils
The simplest way to add colour is with coloured pencils. Some can be blended with water to turn them into watercolours. You can also layer coloured pencils on top of each other to make new colours.

Pencils
Soft pencils have the letter 'B' on them and make black, smudgy lines. Hard pencils have the letter 'H' on them, and make light, thin lines.

Hard pencil

Soft pencil

Paper
Try using different papers such as cartridge paper, tissue paper and sugar paper to add extra texture to your drawings.

Corrugated paper adds extra depth to bumpy textures

Charcoal and chalk

Charcoal comes in black, brittle sticks, which can be smudged and blended easily to create shadowy, dramatic pictures. Chalk pastels are good for adding highlights, and are best used on coloured paper.

Felt-tip pens

Pens can be used to add a more cartoon-ish feel to your drawings. You can use them to define outlines and create dramatic patterns and markings.

Other equipment

Firm erasers will rub out most pencil and some coloured pencil marks. Kneadable erasers (putty rubbers) can be squashed into all sorts of shapes to 'lift' marks off the page. A good pencil sharpener is useful. Use paintbrushes to add water to water-soluble coloured pencils.

Buy handmade paper from gift or art shops

Textured papers make excellent backgrounds.

Shading

To make your dinosaurs look three dimensional, you'll need to add dark shading and white highlights to your drawings. These are called tones.

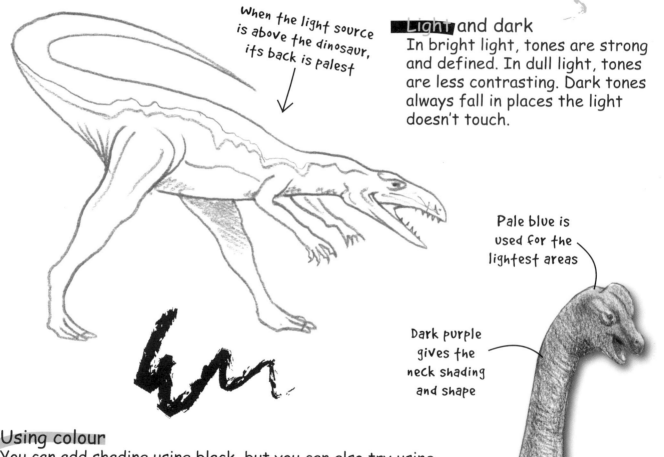

When the light source is above the dinosaur, its back is palest

Light and dark

In bright light, tones are strong and defined. In dull light, tones are less contrasting. Dark tones always fall in places the light doesn't touch.

Pale blue is used for the lightest areas

Dark purple gives the neck shading and shape

Using colour

You can add shading using black, but you can also try using other dark colours, such as dark blue or brown. Highlights can be created using white or by leaving areas of blank paper, but you can also use any pale shade that contrasts with the main body colour — try yellow and pale blue.

Brown is used for the dark areas

8

Highlights

To give your drawings depth, add highlights to areas of deep colours so that they contrast brightly. You can create highlights by leaving areas of white paper empty or colouring over with white pastel or coloured pencil.

Leaving pale patches in dark-coloured areas makes the surface look shiny

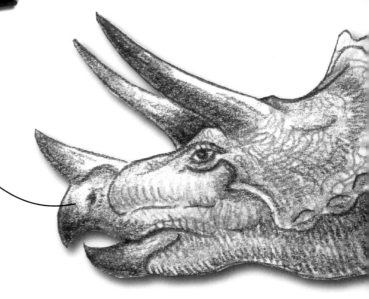

Hatching

Draw thicker lines, closer together to create dark tones, and further apart to make light tones.

Crosshatching

For darker shading, draw hatching lines that cross each other. Closer lines make darker tones.

Stippling

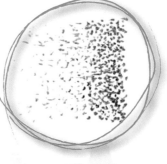

Draw dots close together for dark tones and further apart for lighter tones.

Triple tone

To create delicate shading that looks realistic, your areas of shadow should progress from light to dark gradually. Go over the darkest areas again, pressing harder, and then press more gently as you reach the medium areas to blend light and dark.

Shading goes gradually from light to dark

9

Texture

TEXTURE IS THE WAY SOMETHING FEELS WHEN IT IS TOUCHED. DINOSAURS WERE REPTILES, SO MOST OF THEM PROBABLY HAD BUMPY, SCALY SKIN. HERE'S HOW YOU CAN CREATE TEXTURE IN YOUR DRAWINGS.

Scales and wrinkles

To make the textures you draw on your dinosaurs look realistic, don't draw every single scale or bump. Add lots of detail on the parts of the dinosaur that are nearest, and more sketchy detail on the parts that are furthest away.

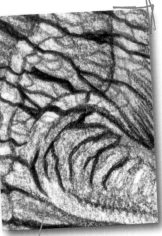

Scales

Add overlapping circular pencil marks over white paper or a base colour.

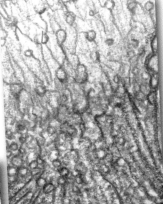

Feathers

Draw lots of tiny lines, all going in the same direction.

Bumps

Use a sharpened pencil to draw thin wavy lines and small circles.

Wrinkles

Draw your base colours, then use a black pencil to create thick lines that criss-cross one another.

10

Patterned skin

It is thought that many dinosaurs had markings on their skin to help them blend into their surroundings.

Mottled colours

Use two colours to make the base colour. Then use darker versions of both colours to draw lines of shadow over the top.

Stripes

Bold, scribbly stripes in a colour that contrasts with the main body colour look dramatic.

DRAW TEXTURES IN THE DIRECTIONS THEY GROW OR APPEAR, AND MAKE THEM DARKER IN DARK-TONED AREAS. NEVER TRY TO DRAW ALL THE TEXTURES YOU SEE, BUT LEAVE THE HIGHLIGHTED AREAS WITHOUT ANY MARKS.

perspective

OBJECTS SEEM SMALLER TO THE VIEWER THE MORE DISTANT THEY ARE. THIS MEANS THAT AN OBJECT IN THE FOREGROUND OF A DRAWING SHOULD APPEAR BIGGER THAN AN OBJECT IN THE BACKGROUND. THIS IS KNOWN AS PERSPECTIVE.

Colour

Use bright colours on the areas of your subject closest to the viewer, and paler colours on the parts that are further away to create the impression of distance.

From the side, Polacanthus' head looks quite small, but its body is massive.

Foreshortening

When drawing a dinosaur walking towards you, the parts that are closest, such as the head, will seem much bigger than they really are compared to the rest of the body. This is called foreshortening.

From the front, the head and front legs look much bigger.

Action

SOME DINOSAURS WERE SPEEDY HUNTERS, WHILE OTHERS SLOWLY PLODDED THE EARTH. HERE'S SOME IDEAS TO GET ALL KINDS OF DINOSAURS MOVING.

Movement lines show that Spinosaurus is whipping its tail quickly back and forth

Once you have drawn your dinosaur, try smudging chalk pastels around the outline or drawing broken lines to give the idea of movement.

To draw a heavy, lumbering dinosaur, make the tones closest to the ground as dark as you can. This helps to make the dinosaur look heavy.

13

Brachiosaurus

1 Draw a large oval body, with four thick legs, a long neck and a small round head.

The head is a tiny circle compared to the body

Draw a curving 'J' shape for a tail

2 Shape the legs and neck using curving lines. Add the snout and the eye.

curve the neck

Thicken the tail to fit on the oval body

3 To show tone, lightly hatch little lines where the light does not reach.

Add a crest to the head and draw the open mouth

Don't forget the toenails

4 Add colour using soft blues and greys. Make the skin look textured by drawing in rough horizontal strokes over the base colour.

Shadowy areas are dark, with highlights of reddish-pink

Try working on dark paper, drawing shadows in black and dark purple, and highlights in white and pale blue.

Allosaurus

1 Draw the body and legs as a collection of triangles, and add a curving tail.

The leg behind is smaller than the leg in front

2 Add curves around the outside of your guidelines. The curve at the back of the head is similar to the curve of the back.

3 Rub out the guidelines and add details — the claws, mouth, eye and the ridges on top of the snout.

4 Show tone and texture using light pencil marks, leaving the paper white where the light is shining.

5 Colour your drawing using green, then add orange to highlight. Use slightly rough markings on the body to show the scaly texture of the skin.

Try drawing on textured paper. Use blunt pencils to create a base colour. Then use a brown pencil to add circular shapes and squiggly lines on top.

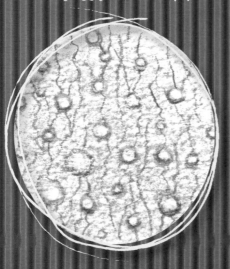

Herrerasaurus

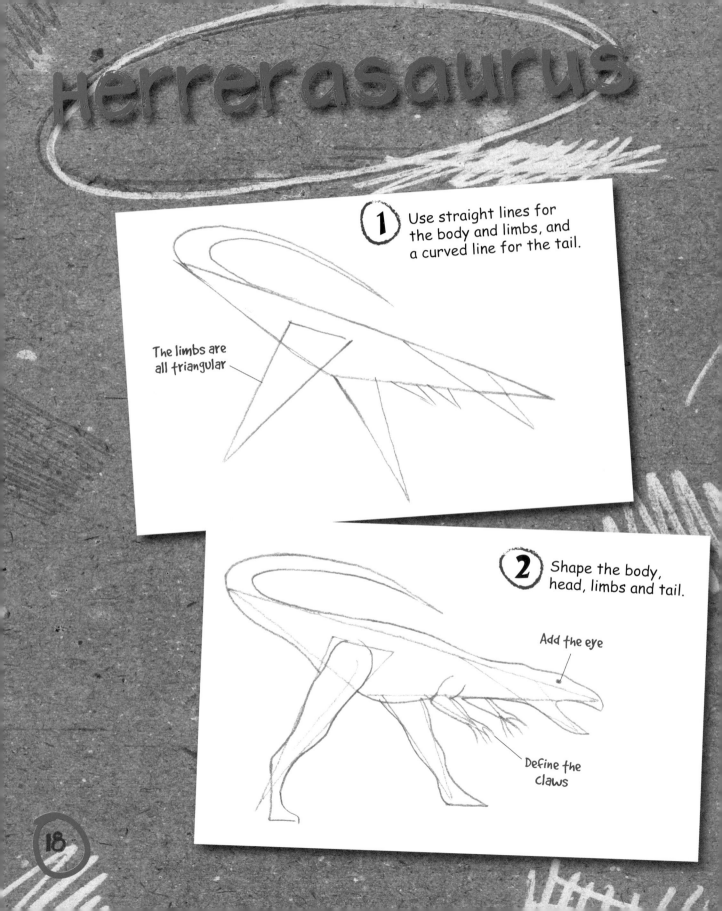

1 Use straight lines for the body and limbs, and a curved line for the tail.

The limbs are all triangular

2 Shape the body, head, limbs and tail.

Add the eye

Define the claws

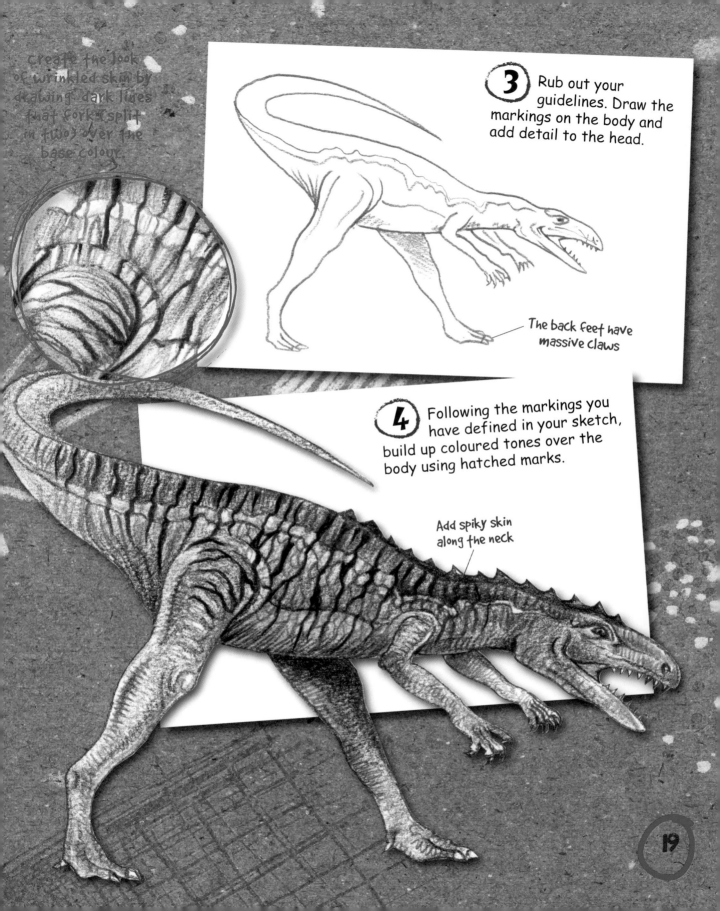

Create the look of wrinkled skin by drawing dark lines that fork (split in two) over the base colour.

3 Rub out your guidelines. Draw the markings on the body and add detail to the head.

The back feet have massive claws

4 Following the markings you have defined in your sketch, build up coloured tones over the body using hatched marks.

Add spiky skin along the neck

19

1 Draw a triangle for the body. Add lines for the neck, limbs and tail and draw a small circle for the head.

This leg is raised so it is drawn as two triangles

2 Soften the curve of the back and body. Shape the neck, tail and limbs around your guidelines. Draw the beak, and three claws at the end of each limb.

The neck gets slightly thicker as it joins the body

The back leg is large and powerful

3 Show texture by drawing lines to show the muscles on the neck, body and tail. Shade the darker areas and add detail to the features.

Shape the legs

4 Blend colours, working from dark blue on the back to yellow for the belly. Use your pencil to add a few circular scales and spots.

Dilophosaurus

1 Draw the basic ovals for the head and body, and triangles for the limbs.

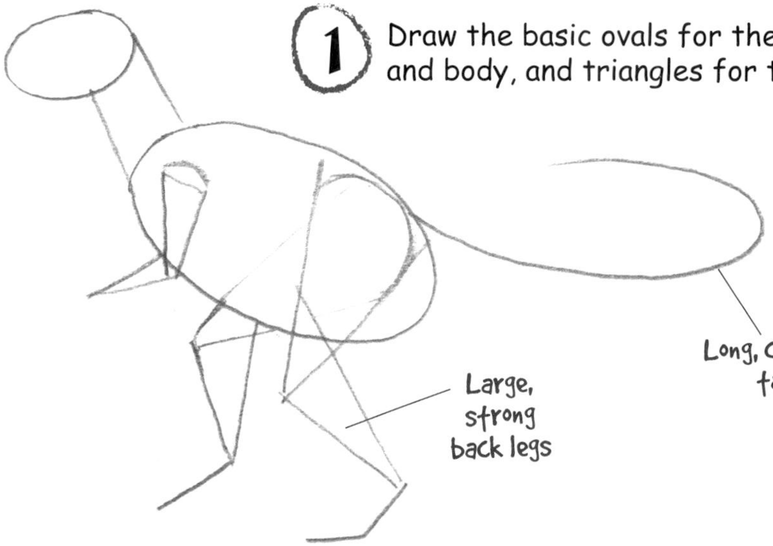

Long, curving tail

Large, strong back legs

2 Fill out the guidelines with curving lines. The mouth is open and there are two long crests on top of the head.

The tail is very thick where it joins the body

3 Draw the eyes — they are quite far back on the head. Build up the curved shapes of the dinosaur. Rub out your earlier guidelines and continue to build up details and tones.

You can add movement to your drawing by making all your lines and shading go in the same direction.

Add the claws

Little hatched lines show dark tones

4 Use blues and purples to add colour. Leave pale areas as highlights at the tops of the crests and limbs, and along the tail.

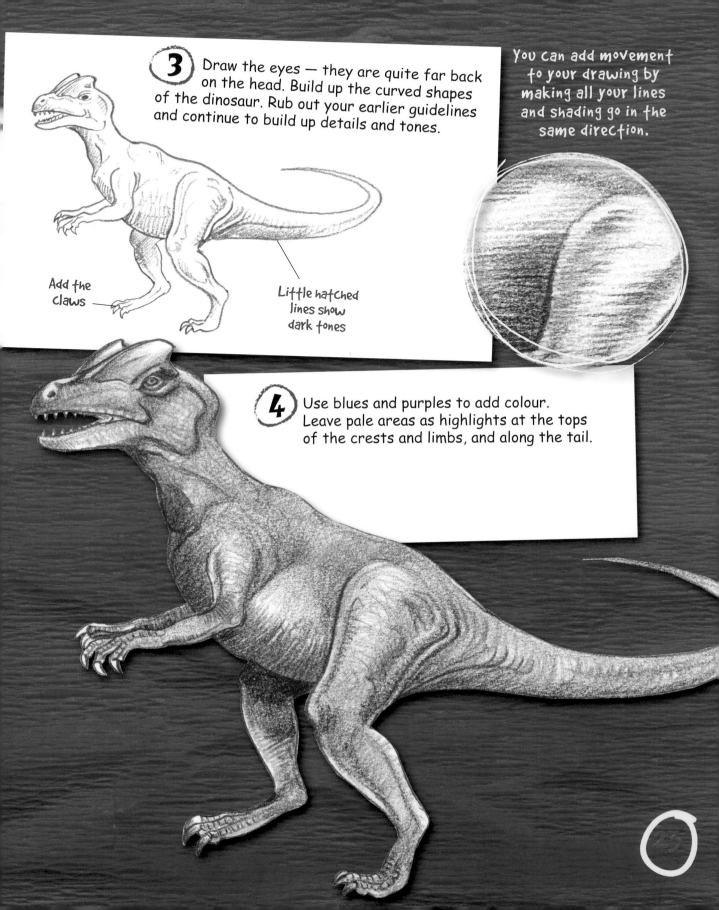

Deinonychus

1 Draw an oval for the body and lines for the neck. Add triangles for the limbs and the head.

The tail is long, and curves away from the body

2 Shape the muscular curves of the legs, and the head with its powerful jaws.

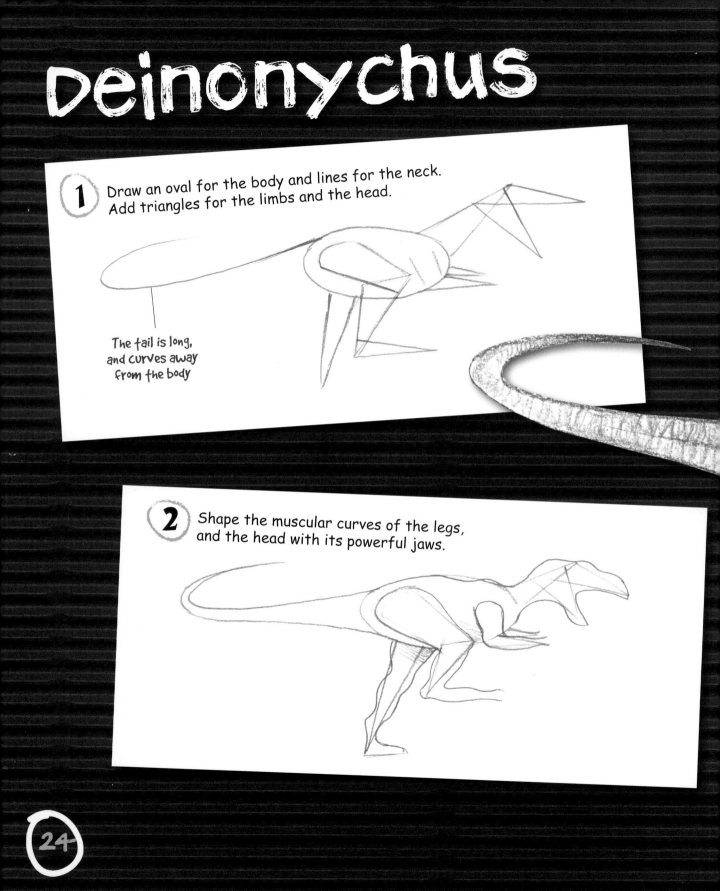

24

3 Add claws and sharp teeth and build up dark tones underneath the body and on the back leg.

Draw the eye

Add the teeth

4 Use a dark orange as a base colour, making it stronger and brighter on the head. Draw the markings in blue on the back and legs.

polacanthus

1 Draw an oval with four straight legs at the bottom, and then add a curved tail at the back.

Draw a point for the head

2 Show the shape of the knee joints on the legs and build up the head shape, keeping the neck the same width.

3 Build up the tones with softly hatched lines on the tops of the legs and the underside of the tail. Start to rub out your guidelines.

Begin to add rows of spikes

Shape the head and add the eye

4 Continue drawing the rows of spikes to the end of the tail. Add a few circles on the body to show the scaly texture.

Darken the shading on the legs

5 Use a soft brown over the lower half of the body. Without pressing hard, colour the back and the top areas of the head and tail using blue. With the same pencil, define some of the scales, pressing more firmly.

Colour the spikes cream, and add a brown shadow on each one

Triceratops

1 Draw an oval that ends in a point at one end. Add four legs and a curving tail.

The neck frill starts as a semi-circle

2 Add the horns, and begin to shape the head by drawing the beaklike mouth.

3 Start to shade in the tones and wrinkles under and around the legs. Shape the head and the neck frill.

Draw the eye

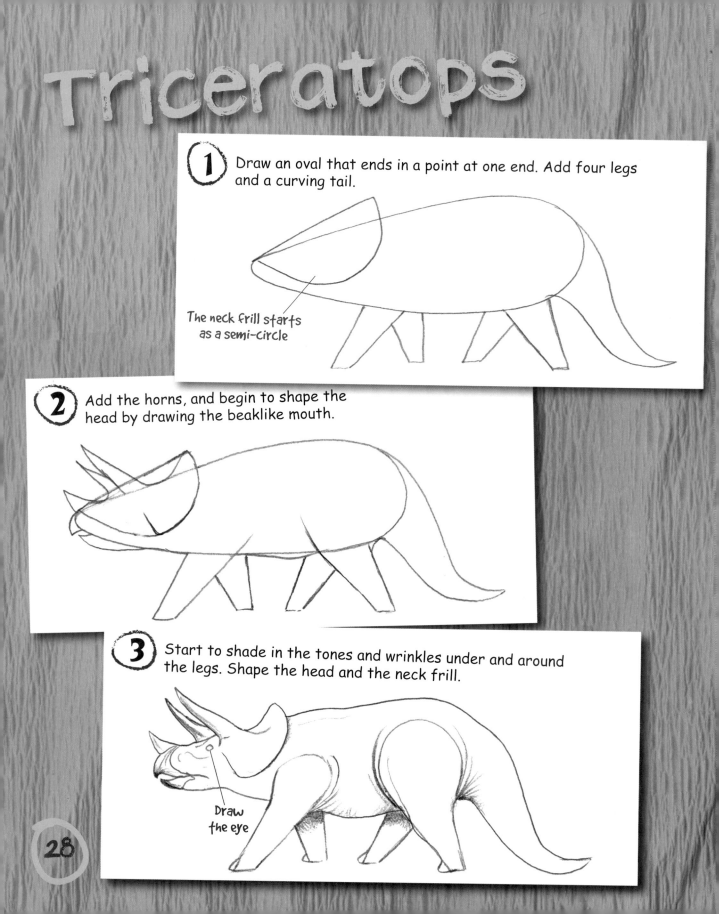

4 Shade the horns to make them look 3D, and add detail to the head and skin.

Create bumpy skin by drawing circles in greens and browns. Then use a sharp pencil to draw lines, following the outlines of parts of the circles.

5 Add colour using greens and blues. Use brown for details and shadows. Leave some pale highlights on the horns and around the mouth.

Ankylosaurus

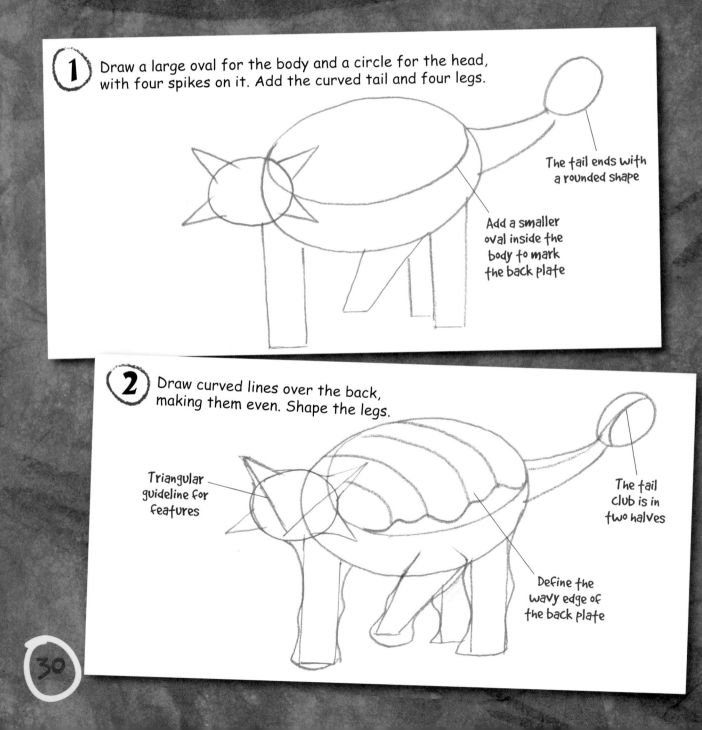

1 Draw a large oval for the body and a circle for the head, with four spikes on it. Add the curved tail and four legs.

The tail ends with a rounded shape

Add a smaller oval inside the body to mark the back plate

2 Draw curved lines over the back, making them even. Shape the legs.

Triangular guideline for features

The tail club is in two halves

Define the wavy edge of the back plate

3 Add rows of spikes on the back plate. Draw the detail on the head and shade the body and legs.

The spikes that are furthest away are smallest

Short stubby claws

4 Make the body orange and the back plate blue. The spikes are bone-coloured with brown shadows.

Colour in small circles, pressing quite hard to create the rough texture

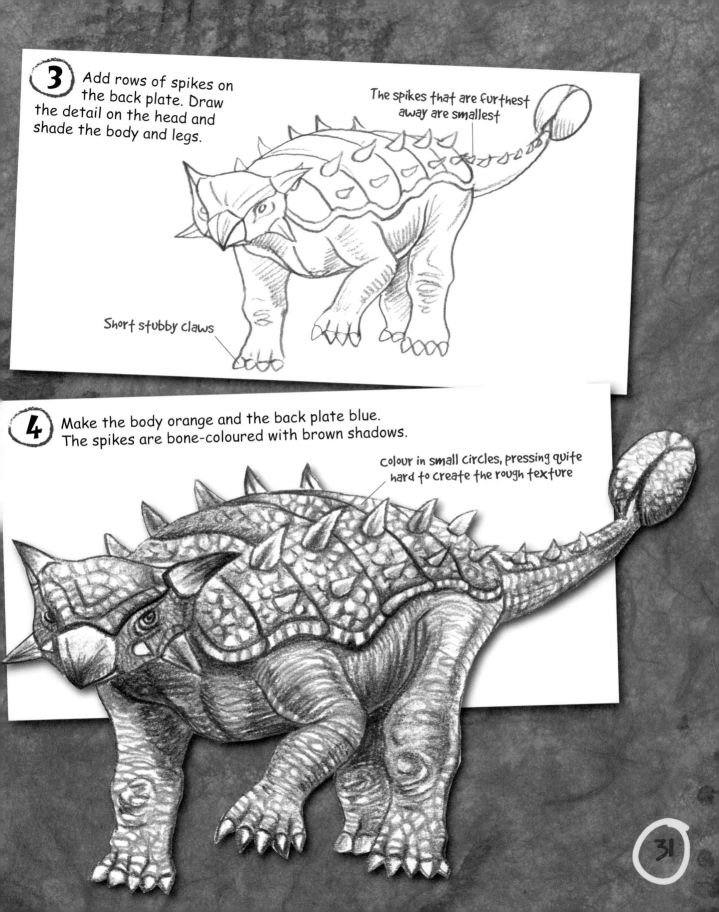

velociraptor

1 Draw a rounded body and a curving tail. Create the head and limbs using triangular shapes.

2 Draw the long, flat snout, pointed toes and curved neck.

Shape the jaws

3 Rub out the guides and add detail and tone with soft lines. Draw the teeth and claws.

Darken features

This line adds perspective to the tail

Try using watercolour pencils to colour in the markings. Then wet a thin brush and go over your colours gently, blending them slightly.

4 Colour in, following the markings you have sketched. Make your shading paler on the head.

33

Spinosaurus

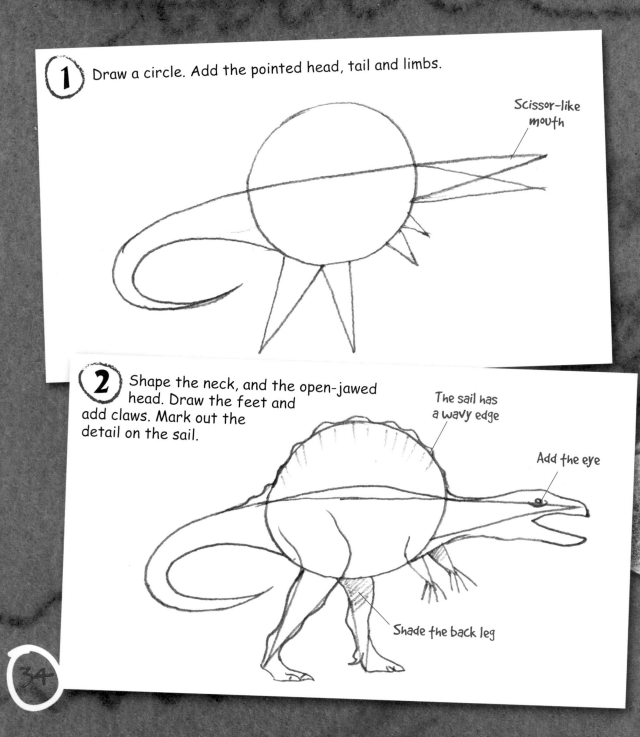

1 Draw a circle. Add the pointed head, tail and limbs.

Scissor-like mouth

2 Shape the neck, and the open-jawed head. Draw the feet and add claws. Mark out the detail on the sail.

The sail has a wavy edge

Add the eye

Shade the back leg

3 Draw the patterned skin using soft pencil marks. Rub out the guidelines and shape the head.

4 Add colour using purple and red, following your markings. Add highlights in pale orange.

35

Parasaurolophus

1 Draw an oval for the body and add legs and a triangular head.

The tail curves away

2 Shape the legs and the pointy head with its long crest.

Draw triangular front limbs

3 Add detail to the head and begin to shade in darker areas. Erase your guidelines.

Begin to shape the front limbs

4 Draw the pattern on the skin and add more wrinkles and shading to the underside of the body and neck.

Pointed claws

5 Use orange for the base colour. Over this, draw lines of scribbles in green, red and yellow from the neck down the length of the body.

compsognathus

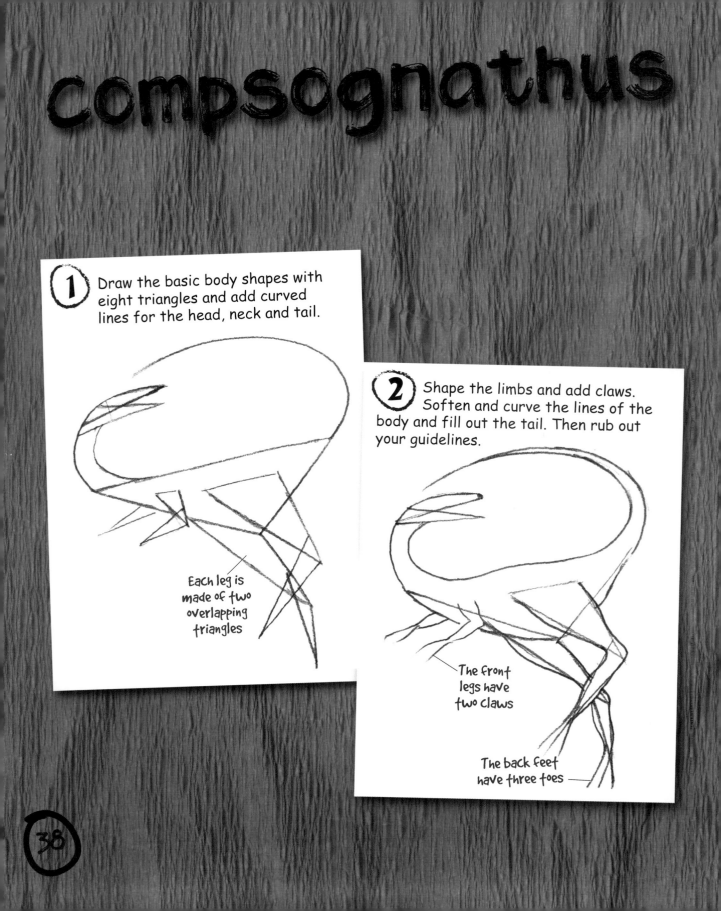

1 Draw the basic body shapes with eight triangles and add curved lines for the head, neck and tail.

Each leg is made of two overlapping triangles

2 Shape the limbs and add claws. Soften and curve the lines of the body and fill out the tail. Then rub out your guidelines.

The front legs have two claws

The back feet have three toes

3 Add shading with hatched lines. Show feathers by using short lines to blur the outline of the back, head and tail.

Add detail to the head

Shade the back leg

4 Create the look of fur by colouring using lots of short strokes, all going in the same direction.

To achieve a feathery texture draw short, soft pencil lines in different colours all going roughly the same way. Then use a very sharp pencil to add tiny lines to some feathers.

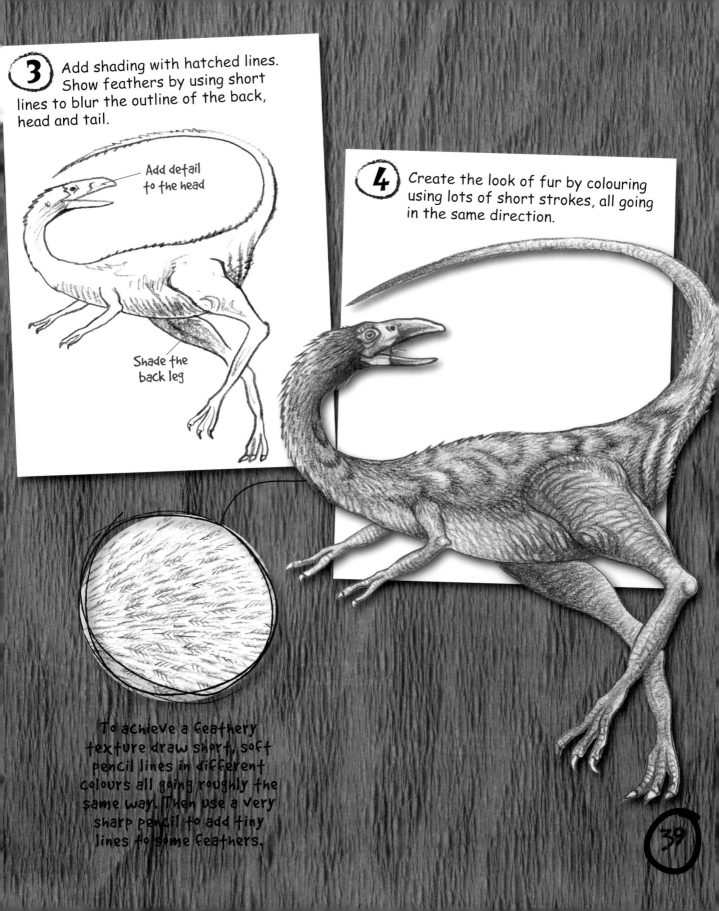

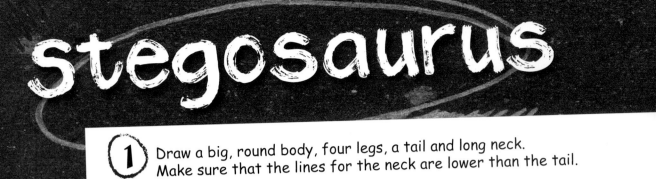

stegosaurus

1 Draw a big, round body, four legs, a tail and long neck.
Make sure that the lines for the neck are lower than the tail.

The front legs are
much smaller than
the back legs

2 Create the back plates as
triangles. Shape the head and
add detail. Draw the claws.

Lines here show the
muscles on the neck

Slender
head

3 Shape the plates along the back and tail. Draw four spikes at the end of the tail.

4 Use shading and colour to make the skin look scaly. Use blue and green on the top of the body and yellow and red for the plates and belly. Layer dark blue over green with touches of black in the darkest places.

Try drawing your dinosaur on pale green paper. Then create the look of textured skin by drawing wiggly lines in blue, dark green and orange over the top.

Tyrannosaurus

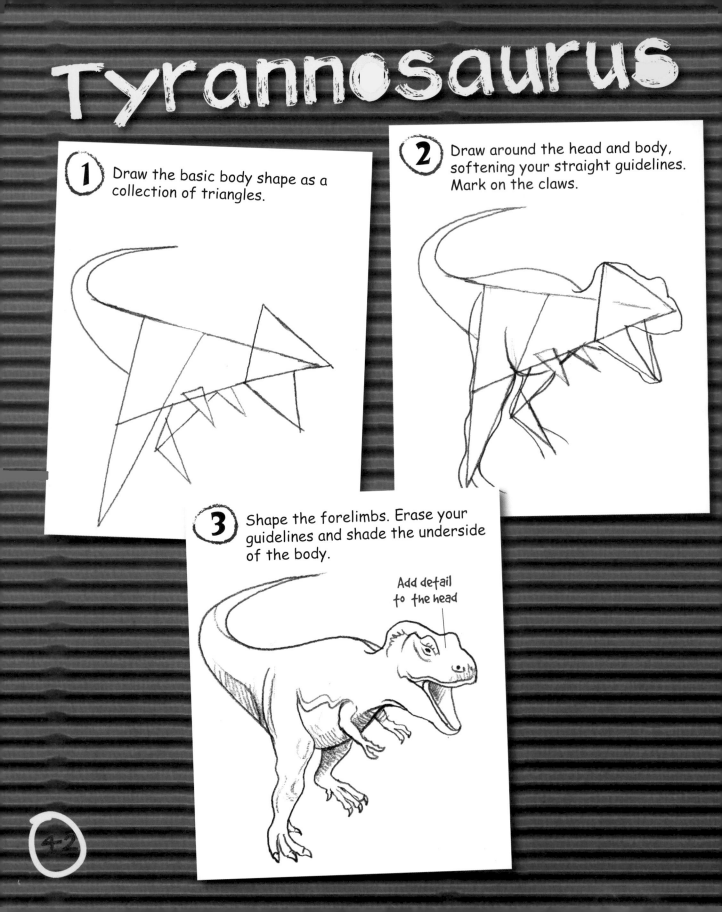

1 Draw the basic body shape as a collection of triangles.

2 Draw around the head and body, softening your straight guidelines. Mark on the claws.

3 Shape the forelimbs. Erase your guidelines and shade the underside of the body.

Add detail to the head

42

Try softly shading thick lines that cross each other to create these markings.

4 Add ridges along the back. Build up wrinkles and shade along the tail.

Add the teeth

Leave the teeth white

5 Use a few different greens to create the base colour. Add detail in brown and use red for the mouth.

Gallery

THERE ARE LOTS OF OTHER DINOSAUR SPECIES, JUST WAITING TO BE DRAWN. HERE ARE SOME IDEAS TO GET YOU STARTED, OR TRY DRAWING THE ONES YOU'VE ALREADY ENCOUNTERED IN NEW POSES.

Giganotosaurus

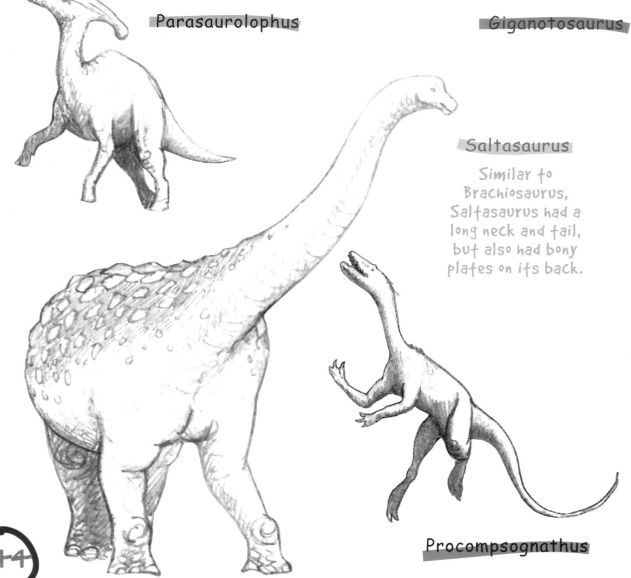

Parasaurolophus

Saltasaurus

Similar to Brachiosaurus, Saltasaurus had a long neck and tail, but also had bony plates on its back.

Procompsognathus

44

Coelophysis

Maiasaura

Psittacosaurus

Eustreptospondylus

You can put any predator dinosaur in this pose to make it look speedy.

45

Yunnanosaurus

Herrerasaurus

Make carnivores look
fierce by drawing
them with their
powerful jaws open
to show their teeth.

Riojasaurus

46

Spinosaurus

Triceratops

Shunosaurus

Caudipteryx

Edmontonia

4-7

First published in 2007 by Bardfield Press
Copyright © Miles Kelly Publishing Ltd 2007

Bardfield Press is an imprint of Miles Kelly Publishing Ltd,
Bardfield Centre, Great Bardfield, Essex, CM7 4SL

2 4 6 8 10 9 7 5 3 1

EDITORIAL DIRECTOR Belinda Gallagher
ART DIRECTOR Jo Brewer
EDITOR Rosalind McGuire
DESIGNER Candice Bekir
REPROGRAPHICS Anthony Cambray,
Stephan Davis, Liberty Newton, Ian Paulyn
PRODUCTION MANAGER Elizabeth Brunwin

ISBN 978-1-84236-829-9

Printed in China

British Library Cataloguing-in-Publication Data
A catalogue record for this book is available from the British Library

www.mileskelly.net
info@mileskelly.net